CH

War Memorials

USS Arizona
MEMORIAL

USS ARIZONA BB 39

Maureen Picard Robins

ROURKE PUBLISHING
Vero Beach, Florida 32964

www.rourkepublishing.com

Photo credits: © U.S. Department of Defense: Title Page, 5, 14, 15, 16, 17, 20, 21, 23, 24, 25, 28, 29; © Wikipedia: 4, 18, 24; © Julie Ridge: 7; © National Park Service: 7, 8, 10, 19; © Library of Congress: 7, 13; © US Airforce: 9; © US Army: 9; © US Navy: 11, 22; © Brett Seymour NPS: 12, 26, 27, 28 © Associated Press: 18; © US Naval Historical Center: 19; © National Archives: 19; © Stephen Walls: borders

Editor: Kelli Hicks

Cover and Interior design by Tara Raymo

Library of Congress Cataloging-in-Publication Data

Robins, Maureen Picard.
  USS Arizona Memorial / Maureen Picard Robins.
      p. cm. -- (War memorials)
  Includes index.
  ISBN 978-1-60694-429-5
  1. USS Arizona Memorial (Hawaii)--Juvenile literature. 2. Arizona
(Battleship)--Juvenile literature. 3. Pearl Harbor (Hawaii), Attack on,
1941--Juvenile literature. 4. World War, 1939-1945--United States--Hawaii--Juvenile
literature. I. Title.
  D835.H3R63 2010
  940.54'659693--dc22
                                     2009005887

Printed in the USA

CG/CG

ROURKE PUBLISHING

www.rourkepublishing.com - rourke@rourkepublishing.com
Post Office Box 643328 Vero Beach, Florida 32964

Table of Contents

YESTERDAY, DECEMBER 7, 1941 - A DATE WHICH WILL LIVE IN **INFAMY** - THE UNITED STATES OF AMERICA WAS SUDDENLY AND DELIBERATELY ATTACKED BY NAVAL AND AIR FORCES OF THE EMPIRE OF JAPAN. THE ATTACK YESTERDAY ON THE HAWAIIAN ISLANDS HAS CAUSED SEVERE DAMAGE TO AMERICAN NAVAL AND MILITARY FORCES. VERY MANY AMERICAN LIVES HAVE BEEN LOST. ALWAYS WE WILL REMEMBER THE CHARACTER OF THE ONSLAUGHT AGAINST US. NO MATTER HOW LONG IT MAY TAKE US TO OVERCOME THIS PREMEDITATED INVASION, THE AMERICAN PEOPLE IN THEIR RIGHTEOUS MIGHT WILL WIN THROUGH TO ABSOLUTE VICTORY.

President Franklin Delano Roosevelt, December 8, 1941

A Watery Grave

On December 7, 1941, the *USS Arizona* was **moored** alongside 17 other American battleships at Pearl Harbor, Hawaii. The world was not at peace. In Europe, Germany, with Adolf Hitler as its Fuhrer, attacked France and Great Britain. In Asia, Japan was at war with China and wanted to take over other islands in the Pacific.

Pearl Harbor is on the island of Oahu in Hawaii and currently serves as the headquarters for the U.S. Pacific Fleet.

But on a bright and beautiful morning in December, five bombs dropped from 9,500 feet (2,895.6 meters) in the air. One of the bombs, weighing 1,760 pounds (798.32 kilograms), slammed into the deck of the *USS Arizona*. It separated the **bow** from the rest of the ship and lifted the 33 thousand ton **vessel** out of the water.

The bombs created an explosion that **ignited** the ship's fuel stores and gun powder.

In fewer than nine minutes the ship sank in an upright position. It burned for three days and took the lives of 1,177 sailors. The fire so hot, the destruction so complete, few bodies were ever recovered.

The ship became a watery grave.

In 1917, The United States Army and Navy began to use Pearl Harbor as a military outpost.

America Enters World War II

The day after the attacks, President Franklin Delano Roosevelt appeared to speak before a joint session of Congress. After that speech, Congress declared that the United States was at war with Japan. Three days later, Germany and Italy declared war on the United States.

Germany, Japan, and Italy signed an agreement to become the Axis
Alliance. The pact promised joint action if any of the three nations
went to war with the U.S.

Why a Memorial?

At the end of World War II many Americans saw a need to pay tribute and remember those who perished during the attacks at Pearl Harbor. The *USS Arizona* site itself had become a gravesite for over 1,000 men.

Many people believed a symbol of the attacks was needed. A symbol would help people remember how Americans were caught unaware during a time the world was at war and how they were able to turn their bad luck into victory.

In 1946, Tucker Gratz, a well-known Hawaiian businessman organized an effort to create a shrine to the sunken ship. These efforts lead to the creation of the Pacific War Memorial Commission in 1949.

In 1950, Admiral Arthur Radford, the Commander in Chief of the Pacific Fleet ordered construction of a wooden platform and a flag mast on the boat deck of the ship. Every day the flag was raised and lowered. He also asked the government to fund the creation of a permanent memorial, but no funds were available. Eventually, in 1958, President Eisenhower signed a law authorizing the creation of the *USS Arizona* Memorial.

The Design

The navy had a vision for the memorial. The proposed memorial was to resemble a bridge and it was not to touch the remains of the ship. It would also need to hold up to 200 visitors at a time.

The navy also wanted the architecture to be more than just a building; its architecture had to symbolize something.

Ninety-six architects submitted proposals to a committee made up of navy personnel and the Pacific War Memorial Commission. The work of Honolulu-based architect Alfred Pries was accepted.

Pries was an interesting choice of designer. He was a **refugee** from Austria and right after the Pearl Harbor attacks he was placed in an internment camp with the Germans, Italians, and Japanese.

The first drawings included submerged viewing areas where visitors could see the sunken ship through portholes. The navy did not approve that design and Preis was sent back to the drawing board.

The architect returned with an open plan for the interior and an idea for a building with a very unique shape.

Wreaths situated throughout create a somber mood at the memorial.

15

The roofline of the structure would sink at its center and rise at either end. The dip in the roof, it is said, represents the low point for America during World War II, specifically the attack on Pearl Harbor.

The rising roofline at either end represents the Americans soaring to victory. There are also 21 large open spaces in the structure's sides and roof. Those large open spaces represent a continual 21-gun salute to honor the men who perished.

Visitors toss leis into the oil-stained water around the memorial. A legend states that the oil is actually black tears cried by the USS Arizona.

Did you know?

During the construction of the memorial some of the wreckage was removed and stored at a navy facility on Waipio peninsula.

After the Japanese bombed Pearl Harbor, they captured Guam on December 13, 1941, Hong Kong on December 24, Manila on January 2, 1942, and Singapore on February 15. Americans began to fear that the Japanese would try to invade the West Coast and that perhaps the Japanese who lived in America would try to aid them. As a result President Roosevelt issued Executive Order 9066 on February 19, 1942. This authorized the arrest and forced relocation of thousands of Japanese to work camps.

Its net was wide enough to also include residents who were of Italian or German descent.

18

Did you know?

USS stands for United States Ship.

Did you know?

Elvis Presley helped raise money for the memorial by performing a benefit concert on March 25, 1961. The concert generated $54,678.73 — more than ten percent of the $515,728.37 needed to construct the monument.

Did you know?

There were 37 confirmed sets of brothers assigned to the USS Arizona on December 7.

A Tour of the Memorial

Today more than one million visitors a year head to the *USS Arizona* Memorial. The tour begins on land at the visitor center which opened in 1980. There, visitors can view films in one of two 150-seat theaters, observe **artifacts** in a museum, participate in exhibits outlining the events of the Pearl Harbor Attack and reflect at the Remembrance Circle.

From there, visitors take a short boat ride to the memorial itself. Many visitors toss photographs, flower garlands, wreaths or **leis** into the rainbow, oil-streaked water just above the skeleton of the *USS Arizona*.

The memorial is a white, concrete structure that arches over the sunken mid-section of the battleship but does not touch it. From the outside, the 184-foot (56.08 meters) memorial features a unique shape. The roofline sinks in the center then soars upward to both ends.

This aerial photograph shows the shadow of the battleship submerged in the water and the memorial structure that spans its mid-section.

The memorial's interior is divided into three areas.

The Entry Room

The first area holds flags of nine states for which the eight battleships and the *USS Utah* were named. The *USS Utah* still rests in Pearl Harbor. At Pearl Harbor, nine battleships were docked in what was known as Battleship Row. Each of the nine suffered damage in the attacks.

The Assembly Room

This is an open area where ceremonies are held and visitors may reflect and examine the remains of the *USS Arizona* below.

The Shrine Room

This room features a marble plaque with the names of the 1,177 sailors and marines who perished on the *USS Arizona*. This room also honors survivors who have chosen to be buried with their shipmates.

Underwater Is a Living Memorial, Too

A preservation project began in 1982 to find answers to the many questions about the ship. Larry E. Murphy and Daniel Lenihan spent hours underwater around the battleship in an attempt to map and see what was down there. Daniel Lenihan wrote, "It was the biggest object ever mapped by anybody, anywhere in an underwater environment – three times the size of the Statue of Liberty."

The divers were astonished to find that the Number 1 **turret** was in place with its three 14-inch (.36 meters) guns pointing forward. They also found live 5-inch (.13 meters) shells on the deck. Eventually, the team would produce a comprehensive line drawing of the 608-foot (185-meter) battleship.

Another worry about the ship was the amount of oil on board. The ship once contained an estimated 500,000 gallons (1,396 metric tons) of Bunker C fuel oil which had been escaping slowly. The oil is noticeable when visitors throw wreaths and leis into the water surrounding the memorial. It is potentially dangerous for the environment. In addition, investigators want to know about the hull's corroding process and they have developed a team to predict the life span of the boat.

A Living Memorial

Survivors of the attacks at Pearl Harbor may still choose to be buried at the memorial. The *USS Arizona* is a living and changing shrine to those brave Americans who made the ultimate sacrifice in protecting their country.

Timeline

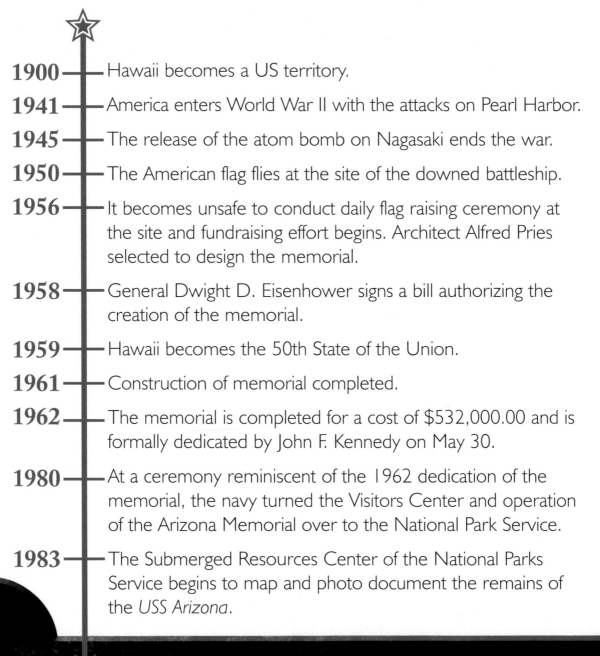

1900 — Hawaii becomes a US territory.

1941 — America enters World War II with the attacks on Pearl Harbor.

1945 — The release of the atom bomb on Nagasaki ends the war.

1950 — The American flag flies at the site of the downed battleship.

1956 — It becomes unsafe to conduct daily flag raising ceremony at the site and fundraising effort begins. Architect Alfred Pries selected to design the memorial.

1958 — General Dwight D. Eisenhower signs a bill authorizing the creation of the memorial.

1959 — Hawaii becomes the 50th State of the Union.

1961 — Construction of memorial completed.

1962 — The memorial is completed for a cost of $532,000.00 and is formally dedicated by John F. Kennedy on May 30.

1980 — At a ceremony reminiscent of the 1962 dedication of the memorial, the navy turned the Visitors Center and operation of the Arizona Memorial over to the National Park Service.

1983 — The Submerged Resources Center of the National Parks Service begins to map and photo document the remains of the *USS Arizona*.

Glossary

artifact (ART-uh-fakt): an object made or changed by human beings

bow (bou): the front of a ship

ignited (ig-NITE): set fire to something

infamy (in-FUH-mee): an evil reputation

lei (lay): a necklace of leaves or flowers

moored (mor): a boat that's tied up or anchored

refugee (REF-yuh-jee): a person who is forced to leave his or her country because of war

turret (TUR-it): a structure on a warship that holds one or more guns

vessel (Vess-uhl): a ship or large boat

Index

Websites

www.pbs.org/perilousfight/battlefield/pearl_harbor

www.pbs.org/childofcamp/history/eo9066.html

www.nps.gov/usar

www.nps.gov/archive/usar/extendweb1.html

About the Author

Maureen Picard Robins writes poetry and books for kids and adults. She is an assistant principal at a New York City middle school. She lives in one of the five boroughs of New York City with her husband and daughters.